W9-BBL-718

Pebble® Plus

Animals Working Together

Moray Eels and Cleaner Shrimp Work Together

by Martha E. H. Rustad

Consulting Editor: Gail Saunders-Smith, PhD

Consultant: Jackie Gai, DVM
Zoo and Exotic Animal Consultation

CAPSTONE PRESS
a capstone imprint

Pebble Plus is published by Capstone Press,
151 Good Counsel Drive, P.O. Box 669, Mankato, Minnesota 56002.
www.capstonepub.com

 Books published by Capstone Press are manufactured with paper containing at least 10 percent post-consumer waste.

Library of Congress Cataloging-in-Publication Data
Rustad, Martha E. H. (Martha Elizabeth Hillman), 1975–
 Moray eels and cleaner shrimp work together / by Martha E. H. Rustad.
  p. cm.—(Pebble plus. Animals working together)
 Includes bibliographical references and index.
 Summary: "Simple text and full-color photographs introduces the symbiotic relationship of moray eels and cleaner shrimp"—Provided by publisher.
 ISBN 978-1-4296-5299-5 (library binding)
 ISBN 978-1-4296-6199-7 (paperback)
 1. Morays—Ecology—Juvenile literature. 2. Shrimps—Ecology—Juvenile literature. 3. Symbiosis—Juvenile literature. I. Title. II. Series.
 QL638.M875R87 2011
 597'.43—dc22   2010025463

Editorial Credits

Erika L. Shores, editor; Bobbie Nuytten, designer; Svetlana Zhurkin, media research;
 Laura Manthe, production specialist

Photo Credits

Alamy/Aquascopic, 16–17; cbimages, 10–11; Reinhard Dirscherl, 6–7; Steven Kovacs, 13
Dreamstime/Exploretimor, 5
Getty Images/Visuals Unlimited/Reinhard Dirscherl, 15
iStockphoto/John Anderson, 19; Zeynep Mufti, 1
Photolibrary/Carol Buchanan, cover, 8–9
Shutterstock/Cigdem Cooper, 20–21

Note to Parents and Teachers

The Animals Working Together series supports national science standards related to biology. This book describes and illustrates the relationship between moray eels and cleaner shrimp. The images support early readers in understanding the text. The repetition of words and phrases helps early readers learn new words. This book also introduces early readers to subject-specific vocabulary words, which are defined in the Glossary section. Early readers may need assistance to read some words and to use the Table of Contents, Glossary, Read More, Internet Sites, and Index sections of the book.

Printed in the United States of America in North Mankato, Minnesota.
092010
005933CGS11

Table of Contents

Symbiosis

An eel pokes its head out

of a coral reef. Its mouth opens,

showing sharp teeth.

A cleaner shrimp crawls in.

Is the shrimp lunch?

No, the shrimp is safe.

It cleans the eel's mouth.

When it's done, it crawls out

and swims away.

Moray eels and cleaner shrimp are animal partners. Each helps the other stay healthy and find food. This relationship is called symbiosis.

Cleaning Time

Moray eels go to cleaner shrimp
for cleanings. The shrimps'
movements tell eels
they're ready. Eels wait
their turn then open wide.

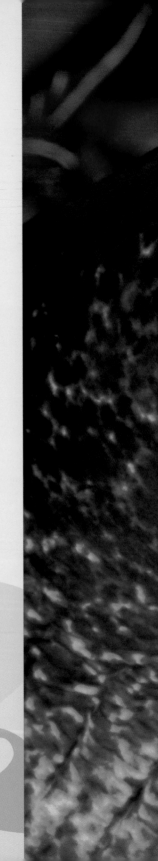

At the end of the cleaning,
moray eels open and close
their mouths. The shrimp know
it's time to get out.

Cleaner Shrimp Help Moray Eels

Moray eels stay healthy
because of cleaner shrimp.
Tiny bits of food get caught
in eels' teeth. Stuck food
might hurt or bother eels.

Cleaner shrimp also clean moray eels' bodies. Parasites stick to eels' skin and gills. These tiny animals can hurt eels.

Moray Eels Help Cleaner Shrimp

Cleaner shrimp eat the food
and parasites they find
on moray eels. In this way,
the shrimp get food
from the eels.

Teamwork

Moray eels and cleaner shrimp are an ocean team.

Symbiosis keeps both animals alive on a coral reef.

Glossary

coral reef—an area of coral skeletons and rocks in shallow ocean water

gill—a body part on the side of a fish; fish use their gills to breathe

parasite—a small organism that lives on or inside an animal or person; parasites sometimes hurt the animal they live on or inside

symbiosis—a relationship between two different kinds of animals; the animals live together to help each other find food, shelter, or safety

Read More

Goldish, Meish. *Moray Eel: Dangerous Teeth*. Afraid of the Water. New York: Bearport, 2010.

Sexton, Colleen A. *Shrimp*. Oceans Alive. Minneapolis: Bellwether Media, 2009.

Silverman, Buffy. *You Scratch My Back*. Raintree Fusion. Chicago: Raintree, 2008.

Internet Sites

FactHound offers a safe, fun way to find Internet sites related to this book. All of the sites on FactHound have been researched by our staff.

Here's all you do:

Visit *www.facthound.com*

Type in this code: 9781429652995

 Check out projects, games and lots more at
www.capstonekids.com

Index

Word Count: 193
Grade: 1
Early-Intervention Level: 17